This
Book
Belongs To:

_____

_____

_____

Date

W9-BFR-729

_____

_____

_____

_____

_____

_____

_____

_____

_____

_____

_____

_____

_____

_____

_____

_____

_____

_____

_____

_____

_____

_____

And wisdom and knowledge shall be the stability of
thy times, and strength of salvation.
Isaiah 33:6

CC

He shall receive the blessing from the Lord,
and righteousness from the God of his salvation.
Psalm 24:5

Shew me thy ways, O Lord;
teach me thy paths.
Psalm 25:4

CC

The Lord preserveth all them that love him.
Psalm 145:20

Wait on the Lord: be of good courage, and he shall
strengthen thine heart: wait, I say, on the Lord.
Psalm 27:14

CC

Nevertheless I am continually with thee: thou hast
holden me by my right hand.
Psalm 73:23

How excellent is thy lovingkindness, O God!
therefore the children of men put their trust under
the shadow of thy wings. Psalm 36:7

Cc

God is our refuge and strength,
a very present help in trouble.
Psalm 46:1

The Lord will give strength unto his people;
the Lord will bless his people with peace.
Psalm 29:11

CC

Be of good courage, and he shall strengthen your
heart, all ye that hope in the Lord.
Psalm 31:24

_____

_____

_____

_____

_____

_____

_____

_____

_____

_____

_____

_____

_____

_____

_____

_____

_____

_____

_____

_____

_____

_____

One thing have I desired of the Lord, that will I seek
after; that I may dwell in the house of the Lord all the
days of my life. Psalm 27:4

CC

Make thy face to shine upon thy servant:
save me for thy mercies' sake.
Psalm 31:16

Unto thee, O Lord, do I lift up my soul.
O my God, I trust in thee.
Psalm 25:1,2

CC

Lead me in thy truth, and teach me: for thou art the
God of my salvation; on thee do I wait all the day.
Psalm 25:5

The law of the Lord is perfect, converting the soul:
the testimony of the Lord is sure,
making wise the simple. Psalm 19:7

CC

The statutes of the Lord are right, rejoicing the heart:
the commandment of the Lord is pure,
enlightening the eyes. Psalm 19:8

The Lord liveth; and blessed be my rock;
and let the God of my salvation be exalted.
Psalm 18:46

The Lord is my rock, and my fortress,
and my deliverer; my God, my strength,
in whom I will trust; Psalm 18:2

Keep me as the apple of the eye, hide me under
the shadow of thy wings.
Psalm 17:8

CC

Thou wilt shew me the path of life: in thy presence is
fulness of joy; at thy right hand there are pleasures
for evermore. Psalm 16:11

But I will hope continually, and will yet
praise thee more and more.
Psalm 71:14

"

The Lord is my light and my salvation;
whom shall I fear? the Lord is the strength of my life;
of whom shall I be afraid? Psalm 27:1

I will rejoice in the Lord, I will joy in
the God of my salvation.
Habakkuk 3:18

CC

Thy mercy, O Lord, is in the heavens;
and thy faithfulness reacheth unto the clouds.
Psalm 36:5

Let, I pray thee, thy merciful kindness be for
my comfort, according to thy word unto thy servant.
Psalm 119:76

CC

Ask, and it shall be given you; seek, and ye shall find;
knock, and it shall be opened unto you.
Matthew 7:7

For if ye forgive men their trespasses,
your heavenly Father will also forgive you.
Matthew 6:14

I will praise thee, O Lord my God, with all my heart:
and I will glorify thy name for evermore.
Psalm 86:12

Every good gift and every perfect gift is from above,
and cometh down from the Father of lights.
James 1:17

Cc

And he said to them all, If any man will come after me,
let him deny himself, and take up his cross daily,
and follow me. Luke 9:23

For even hereunto were ye called: because Christ
also suffered for us, leaving us an example, that ye
should follow his steps: 1Peter 2:21

And whatsoever ye shall ask in my name, that will I do,
that the Father may be glorified in the Son.
John 14:13

And wisdom and knowledge shall be the stability of
thy times, and strength of salvation.
Isaiah 33:6

CC

He shall receive the blessing from the Lord,
and righteousness from the God of his salvation.
Psalm 24:5

Shew me thy ways, O Lord;
teach me thy paths.
Psalm 25:4

The Lord preserveth all them that love him.
Psalm 145:20

Wait on the Lord: be of good courage, and he shall
strengthen thine heart: wait, I say, on the Lord.
Psalm 27:14

CC

Nevertheless I am continually with thee: thou hast
holden me by my right hand.
Psalm 73:23

How excellent is thy lovingkindness, O God!
therefore the children of men put their trust under
the shadow of thy wings. Psalm 36:7

CC

God is our refuge and strength,
a very present help in trouble.
Psalm 46:1

The Lord will give strength unto his people;
the Lord will bless his people with peace.
Psalm 29:11

Cc

Be of good courage, and he shall strengthen your
heart, all ye that hope in the Lord.
Psalm 31:24

One thing have I desired of the Lord, that will I seek
after; that I may dwell in the house of the Lord all the
days of my life. Psalm 27:4

CC

Make thy face to shine upon thy servant:
save me for thy mercies' sake.
Psalm 31:16

_____

_____

_____

_____

_____

_____

_____

_____

_____

_____

_____

_____

_____

_____

_____

_____

_____

_____

_____

_____

_____

_____

_____

_____

Unto thee, O Lord, do I lift up my soul.
O my God, I trust in thee.
Psalm 25:1,2

Lead me in thy truth, and teach me: for thou art the
God of my salvation; on thee do I wait all the day.
Psalm 25:5

_____

_____

_____

_____

_____

_____

_____

_____

_____

_____

_____

_____

_____

_____

_____

_____

_____

_____

_____

_____

_____

_____

_____

The law of the Lord is perfect, converting the soul:
the testimony of the Lord is sure,
making wise the simple. Psalm 19:7

Cc

The statutes of the Lord are right, rejoicing the heart:
the commandment of the Lord is pure,
enlightening the eyes. Psalm 19:8

The Lord liveth; and blessed be my rock;
and let the God of my salvation be exalted.
Psalm 18:46

CC

The Lord is my rock, and my fortress,
and my deliverer; my God, my strength,
in whom I will trust; Psalm 18:2

Keep me as the apple of the eye, hide me under
the shadow of thy wings.
Psalm 17:8

Thou wilt shew me the path of life: in thy presence is
fulness of joy; at thy right hand there are pleasures
for evermore. Psalm 16:11

But I will hope continually, and will yet
praise thee more and more.
Psalm 71:14

The Lord is my light and my salvation;
whom shall I fear? the Lord is the strength of my life;
of whom shall I be afraid? Psalm 27:1

I will rejoice in the Lord, I will joy in
the God of my salvation.
Habakkuk 3:18

Thy mercy, O Lord, is in the heavens;
and thy faithfulness reacheth unto the clouds.
Psalm 36:5

Let, I pray thee, thy merciful kindness be for
my comfort, according to thy word unto thy servant.
Psalm 119:76

CC

Ask, and it shall be given you; seek, and ye shall find;
knock, and it shall be opened unto you.
Matthew 7:7

For if ye forgive men their trespasses,
your heavenly Father will also forgive you.
Matthew 6:14

Cc

I will praise thee, O Lord my God, with all my heart:
and I will glorify thy name for evermore.
Psalm 86:12

Every good gift and every perfect gift is from above,
and cometh down from the Father of lights.
James 1:17

CC

And he said to them all, If any man will come after me,
let him deny himself, and take up his cross daily,
and follow me. Luke 9:23

For even hereunto were ye called: because Christ
also suffered for us, leaving us an example, that ye
should follow his steps: 1Peter 2:21

``

And whatsoever ye shall ask in my name, that will I do,
that the Father may be glorified in the Son.
John 14:13

And wisdom and knowledge shall be the stability of
thy times, and strength of salvation.
Isaiah 33:6

CC

He shall receive the blessing from the Lord,
and righteousness from the God of his salvation.
Psalm 24:5

Shew me thy ways, O Lord;
teach me thy paths.
Psalm 25:4

CC _____

The Lord preserveth all them that love him.
Psalm 145:20

Wait on the Lord: be of good courage, and he shall
strengthen thine heart: wait, I say, on the Lord.
Psalm 27:14

CC

Nevertheless I am continually with thee: thou hast
holden me by my right hand.
Psalm 73:23

_____

_____

_____

_____

_____

_____

_____

_____

_____

_____

_____

_____

_____

_____

_____

_____

_____

_____

_____

_____

_____

How excellent is thy lovingkindness, O God!
therefore the children of men put their trust under
the shadow of thy wings. Psalm 36:7

CC

God is our refuge and strength,
a very present help in trouble.
Psalm 46:1

The Lord will give strength unto his people;
the Lord will bless his people with peace.
Psalm 29:11

Be of good courage, and he shall strengthen your
heart, all ye that hope in the Lord.
Psalm 31:24

One thing have I desired of the Lord, that will I seek
after; that I may dwell in the house of the Lord all the
days of my life. Psalm 27:4

CC

Make thy face to shine upon thy servant:
save me for thy mercies' sake.
Psalm 31:16

Unto thee, O Lord, do I lift up my soul.
O my God, I trust in thee.
Psalm 25:1,2

Lead me in thy truth, and teach me: for thou art the
God of my salvation; on thee do I wait all the day.
Psalm 25:5

The law of the Lord is perfect, converting the soul:
the testimony of the Lord is sure,
making wise the simple. Psalm 19:7

CC

The statutes of the Lord are right, rejoicing the heart:
the commandment of the Lord is pure,
enlightening the eyes. Psalm 19:8

The Lord liveth; and blessed be my rock;
and let the God of my salvation be exalted.
Psalm 18:46

The Lord is my rock, and my fortress,
and my deliverer; my God, my strength,
in whom I will trust; Psalm 18:2

Keep me as the apple of the eye, hide me under
the shadow of thy wings.
Psalm 17:8

CC

Thou wilt shew me the path of life: in thy presence is
fulness of joy; at thy right hand there are pleasures
for evermore. Psalm 16:11

But I will hope continually, and will yet
praise thee more and more.
Psalm 71:14

CC

The Lord is my light and my salvation;
whom shall I fear? the Lord is the strength of my life;
of whom shall I be afraid? Psalm 27:1

I will rejoice in the Lord, I will joy in
the God of my salvation.
Habakkuk 3:18

CC

Thy mercy, O Lord, is in the heavens;
and thy faithfulness reacheth unto the clouds.
Psalm 36:5

Let, I pray thee, thy merciful kindness be for
my comfort, according to thy word unto thy servant.
Psalm 119:76

CC

Ask, and it shall be given you; seek, and ye shall find;
knock, and it shall be opened unto you.
Matthew 7:7

For if ye forgive men their trespasses,
your heavenly Father will also forgive you.
Matthew 6:14

CC

I will praise thee, O Lord my God, with all my heart:
and I will glorify thy name for evermore.
Psalm 86:12

Every good gift and every perfect gift is from above,
and cometh down from the Father of lights.
James 1:17

CC

And he said to them all, If any man will come after me,
let him deny himself, and take up his cross daily,
and follow me. Luke 9:23

For even hereunto were ye called: because Christ
also suffered for us, leaving us an example, that ye
should follow his steps: 1Peter 2:21

CC

And whatsoever ye shall ask in my name, that will I do,
that the Father may be glorified in the Son.
John 14:13

And wisdom and knowledge shall be the stability of
thy times, and strength of salvation.
Isaiah 33:6

CC

He shall receive the blessing from the Lord,
and righteousness from the God of his salvation.
Psalm 24:5

Shew me thy ways, O Lord;
teach me thy paths.
Psalm 25:4

CC

The Lord preserveth all them that love him.
Psalm 145:20

Wait on the Lord: be of good courage, and he shall
strengthen thine heart: wait, I say, on the Lord.
Psalm 27:14

Nevertheless I am continually with thee: thou hast
holden me by my right hand.
Psalm 73:23

How excellent is thy lovingkindness, O God!
therefore the children of men put their trust under
the shadow of thy wings. Psalm 36:7

CC

God is our refuge and strength,
a very present help in trouble.
Psalm 46:1

The Lord will give strength unto his people;
the Lord will bless his people with peace.
Psalm 29:11

Be of good courage, and he shall strengthen your
heart, all ye that hope in the Lord.
Psalm 31:24

One thing have I desired of the Lord, that will I seek
after; that I may dwell in the house of the Lord all the
days of my life. Psalm 27:4

CC

Make thy face to shine upon thy servant:
save me for thy mercies' sake.
Psalm 31:16

Unto thee, O Lord, do I lift up my soul.
O my God, I trust in thee.
Psalm 25:1,2

Lead me in thy truth, and teach me: for thou art the
God of my salvation; on thee do I wait all the day.
Psalm 25:5

The law of the Lord is perfect, converting the soul:
the testimony of the Lord is sure,
making wise the simple. Psalm 19:7

CC

The statutes of the Lord are right, rejoicing the heart:
the commandment of the Lord is pure,
enlightening the eyes. Psalm 19:8

The Lord liveth; and blessed be my rock;
and let the God of my salvation be exalted.
Psalm 18:46

CC

The Lord is my rock, and my fortress,
and my deliverer; my God, my strength,
in whom I will trust; Psalm 18:2

Keep me as the apple of the eye, hide me under
the shadow of thy wings.
Psalm 17:8

CC

Thou wilt shew me the path of life: in thy presence is
fulness of joy; at thy right hand there are pleasures
for evermore. Psalm 16:11

_____

_____

_____

_____

_____

_____

_____

_____

_____

_____

_____

_____

_____

_____

_____

_____

_____

_____

_____

_____

_____

_____

But I will hope continually, and will yet
praise thee more and more.
Psalm 71:14

CC

The Lord is my light and my salvation;
whom shall I fear? the Lord is the strength of my life;
of whom shall I be afraid? Psalm 27:1

I will rejoice in the Lord, I will joy in
the God of my salvation.
Habakkuk 3:18

Thy mercy, O Lord, is in the heavens;
and thy faithfulness reacheth unto the clouds.
Psalm 36:5

Let, I pray thee, thy merciful kindness be for
my comfort, according to thy word unto thy servant.
Psalm 119:76

CC

Ask, and it shall be given you; seek, and ye shall find;
knock, and it shall be opened unto you.
Matthew 7:7

For if ye forgive men their trespasses,
your heavenly Father will also forgive you.
Matthew 6:14

CC

I will praise thee, O Lord my God, with all my heart:
and I will glorify thy name for evermore.
Psalm 86:12

Every good gift and every perfect gift is from above,
and cometh down from the Father of lights.
James 1:17

CC

And he said to them all, If any man will come after me,
let him deny himself, and take up his cross daily,
and follow me. Luke 9:23

For even hereunto were ye called: because Christ
also suffered for us, leaving us an example, that ye
should follow his steps: 1Peter 2:21

CC

And whatsoever ye shall ask in my name, that will I do,
that the Father may be glorified in the Son.
John 14:13

And wisdom and knowledge shall be the stability of
thy times, and strength of salvation.
Isaiah 33:6

CC

He shall receive the blessing from the Lord,
and righteousness from the God of his salvation.
Psalm 24:5

Shew me thy ways, O Lord;
teach me thy paths.
Psalm 25:4

CC

The Lord preserveth all them that love him.
Psalm 145:20

Wait on the Lord: be of good courage, and he shall
strengthen thine heart: wait, I say, on the Lord.
Psalm 27:14

CC

Nevertheless I am continually with thee: thou hast
holden me by my right hand.
Psalm 73:23

How excellent is thy lovingkindness, O God!
therefore the children of men put their trust under
the shadow of thy wings. Psalm 36:7

CC

God is our refuge and strength,
a very present help in trouble.
Psalm 46:1

The Lord will give strength unto his people;
the Lord will bless his people with peace.
Psalm 29:11

CC

Be of good courage, and he shall strengthen your
heart, all ye that hope in the Lord.
Psalm 31:24

One thing have I desired of the Lord, that will I seek
after; that I may dwell in the house of the Lord all the
days of my life. Psalm 27:4

CC

Make thy face to shine upon thy servant:
save me for thy mercies' sake.
Psalm 31:16

Unto thee, O Lord, do I lift up my soul.
O my God, I trust in thee.
Psalm 25:1,2

Lead me in thy truth, and teach me: for thou art the
God of my salvation; on thee do I wait all the day.
Psalm 25:5

The law of the Lord is perfect, converting the soul:
the testimony of the Lord is sure,
making wise the simple. Psalm 19:7

CC

The statutes of the Lord are right, rejoicing the heart:
the commandment of the Lord is pure,
enlightening the eyes. Psalm 19:8

The Lord liveth; and blessed be my rock;
and let the God of my salvation be exalted.
Psalm 18:46

CC

The Lord is my rock, and my fortress,
and my deliverer; my God, my strength,
in whom I will trust; Psalm 18:2

Keep me as the apple of the eye, hide me under
the shadow of thy wings.
Psalm 17:8

Cc

Thou wilt shew me the path of life: in thy presence is
fulness of joy; at thy right hand there are pleasures
for evermore. Psalm 16:11

But I will hope continually, and will yet
praise thee more and more.
Psalm 71:14

The Lord is my light and my salvation;
whom shall I fear? the Lord is the strength of my life;
of whom shall I be afraid? Psalm 27:1

I will rejoice in the Lord, I will joy in
the God of my salvation.
Habakkuk 3:18

Thy mercy, O Lord, is in the heavens;
and thy faithfulness reacheth unto the clouds.
Psalm 36:5

Let, I pray thee, thy merciful kindness be for
my comfort, according to thy word unto thy servant.
Psalm 119:76

CC

Ask, and it shall be given you; seek, and ye shall find;
knock, and it shall be opened unto you.
Matthew 7:7

For if ye forgive men their trespasses,
your heavenly Father will also forgive you.
Matthew 6:14

CC

I will praise thee, O Lord my God, with all my heart:
and I will glorify thy name for evermore.
Psalm 86:12

_____

_____

_____

_____

_____

_____

_____

_____

_____

_____

_____

_____

_____

_____

_____

_____

_____

_____

_____

_____

_____

_____

Every good gift and every perfect gift is from above,
and cometh down from the Father of lights.
James 1:17

And he said to them all, If any man will come after me,
let him deny himself, and take up his cross daily,
and follow me. Luke 9:23

_____

_____

_____

_____

_____

_____

_____

_____

_____

_____

_____

_____

_____

_____

_____

_____

_____

_____

_____

_____

_____

_____

For even hereunto were ye called: because Christ
also suffered for us, leaving us an example, that ye
should follow his steps: 1Peter 2:21

CC

And whatsoever ye shall ask in my name, that will I do,
that the Father may be glorified in the Son.
John 14:13